**SUPER EASY SONGBOOK**

T0055704

Cover photo © Getty Images / Kevin Winter

ISBN 978-1-5400-9420-9

Visit Hal Leonard Online at
**www.halleonard.com**

Contact us:
**Hal Leonard**
7777 West Bluemound Road
Milwaukee, WI 53213
Email: info@halleonard.com

In Europe, contact:
**Hal Leonard Europe Limited**
42 Wigmore Street
Marylebone, London, W1U 2RN
Email: info@halleonardeurope.com

In Australia, contact:
**Hal Leonard Australia Pty. Ltd.**
4 Lentara Court
Cheltenham, Victoria, 3192 Australia
Email: info@halleonard.com.au

# Welcome to the *Super Easy Songbook* series!

## This unique collection will help you play your favorite songs quickly and easily. Here's how it works:

- Play the simplified melody with your right hand. Letter names appear inside each note to assist you.

- There are no key signatures to worry about! If a sharp ♯ or flat ♭ is needed, it is shown beside the note each time.

- There are no page turns, so your hands never have to leave the keyboard.

- If two notes are connected by a tie ⌣, hold the first note for the combined number of beats. (The second note does not show a letter name since it is not re-struck.)

- Add basic chords with your left hand using the provided keyboard diagrams. Chord voicings have been carefully chosen to minimize hand movement.

- The left-hand rhythm is up to you, and chord notes can be played together or separately. Be creative!

- If the chords sound muddy, move your left hand an octave* higher. If this gets in the way of playing the melody, move your right hand an octave higher as well.

  * *An octave spans eight notes. If your starting note is C, the next C to the right is an octave higher.*

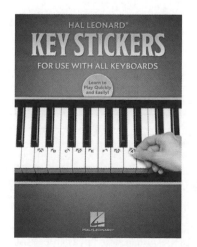

# all the good girls go to hell

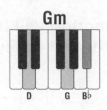
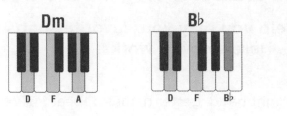
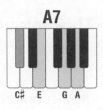

Words and Music by Billie Eilish O'Connell
and Finneas O'Connell

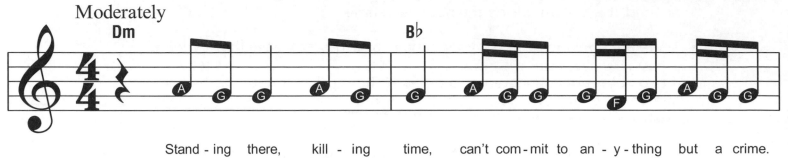

Stand - ing there, kill - ing time, can't com - mit to an - y - thing but a crime.

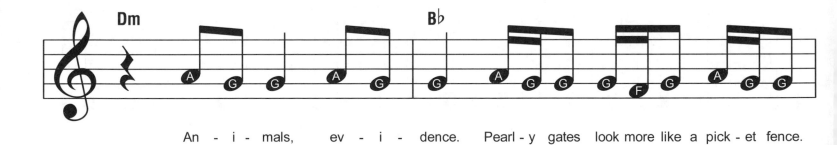

Pe - ter's on va - ca - tion, an o - pen in - vi - ta - tion.

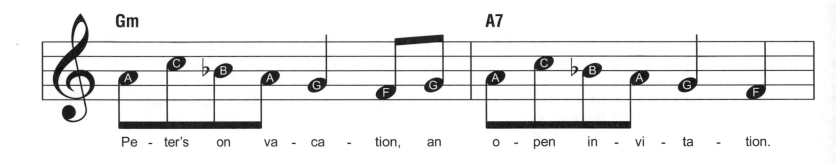

An - i - mals, ev - i - dence. Pearl - y gates look more like a pick - et fence.

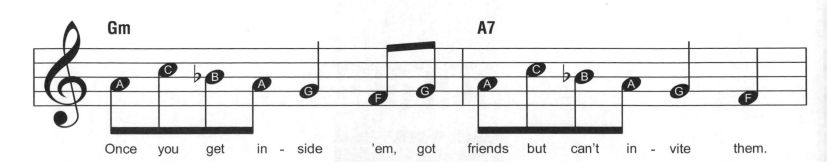

Once you get in - side 'em, got friends but can't in - vite them.

# bad guy

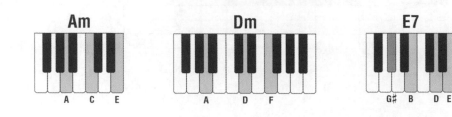

Words and Music by Billie Eilish O'Connell
and Finneas O'Connell

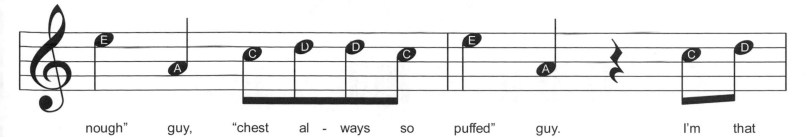

nough" guy, "chest al - ways so puffed" guy. I'm that

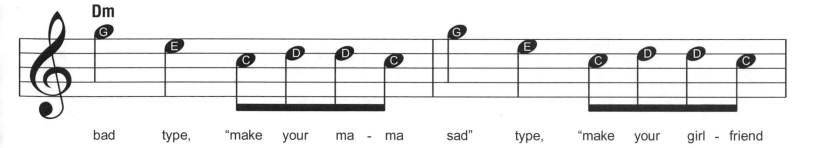

**Dm**

bad type, "make your ma - ma sad" type, "make your girl - friend

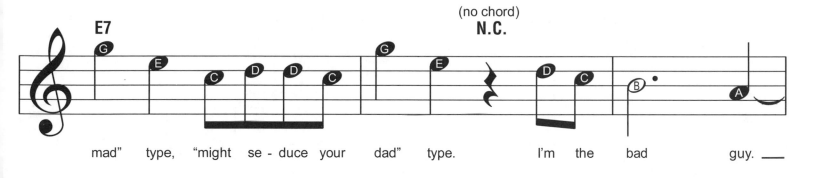

**E7** (no chord) **N.C.**

mad" type, "might se - duce your dad" type. I'm the bad guy. ___

**Am**

___ Duh. *(Instrumental)*

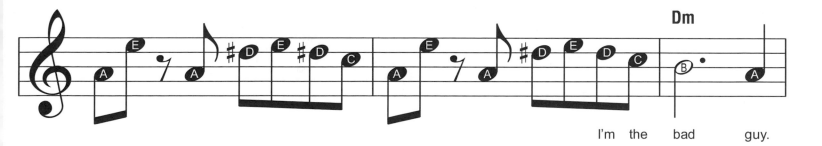

**Dm**

I'm the bad guy.

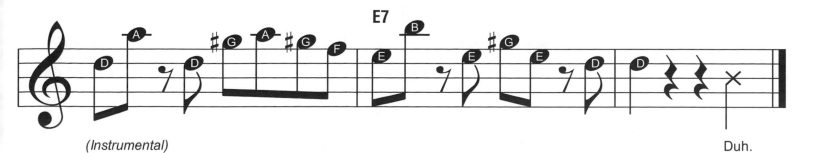

**E7**

*(Instrumental)* Duh.

# bellyache

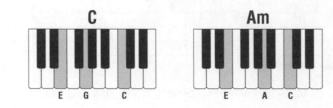
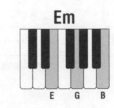

Words and Music by Billie Eilish O'Connell
and Finneas O'Connell

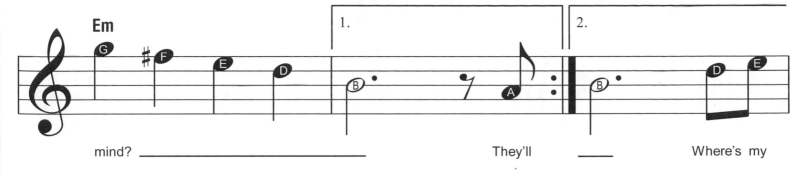

mind? _____ They'll \_\_\_\_ Where's my

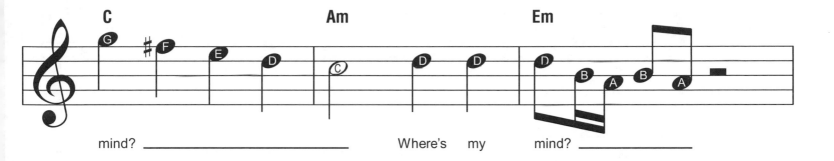

mind? _____ Where's my mind? _____

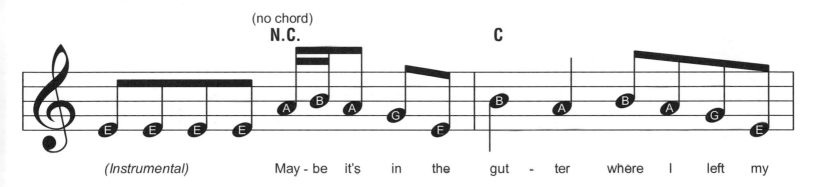

(Instrumental)  May - be it's in the gut - ter where I left my

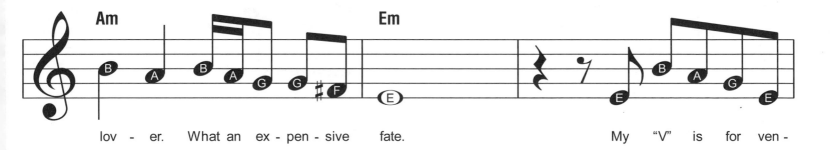

lov - er. What an ex - pen - sive fate. My "V" is for ven -

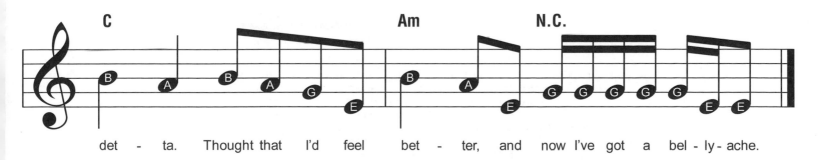

det - ta. Thought that I'd feel bet - ter, and now I've got a bel - ly - ache.

# bored

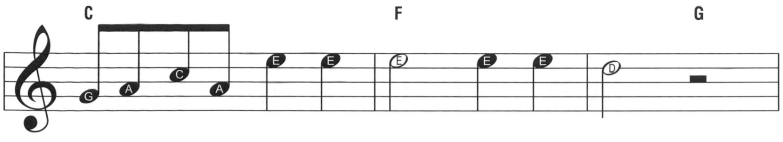

for, giv-ing you what you say I need, say I need.

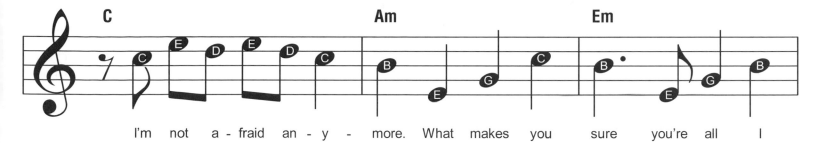

I'm not a-fraid an-y - more. What makes you sure you're all I

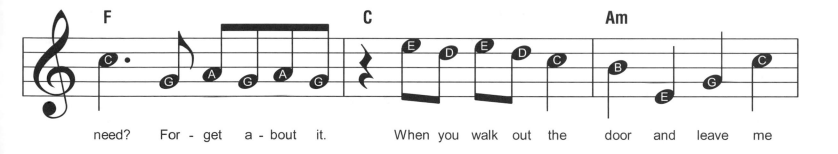

need? For-get a-bout it. When you walk out the door and leave me

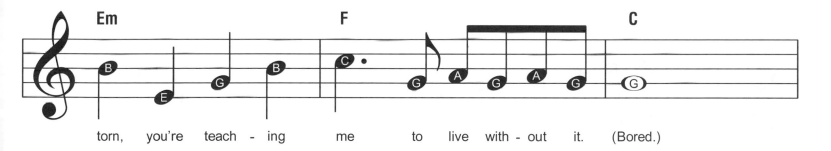

torn, you're teach - ing me to live with-out it. (Bored.)

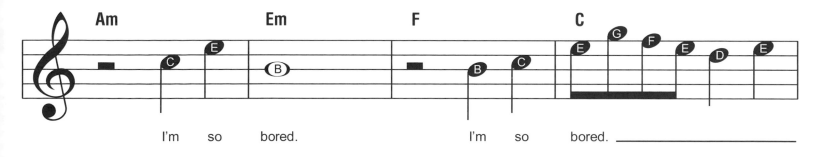

I'm so bored. I'm so bored. _____

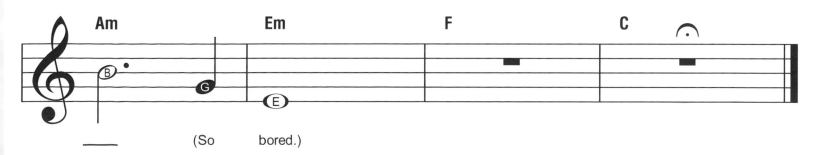

_____ (So bored.)

# copycat

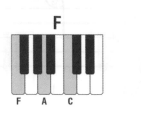
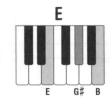
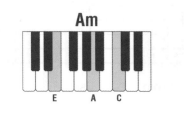

Words and Music by Billie Eilish O'Connell
and Finneas O'Connell

Don't be cau - tious, don't be kind. You com - mit - ted, I'm your crime. ___ Push my but - ton an - y - time. You got your fin - ger on the trig - ger, but your trig - ger fin - ger's mine. ___ Sil - ver dol - lar, gold - en flame. Dirt - y wa - ter, poi - son ___ rain. ___ Per - fect mur - der, take your aim. I don't be -

# 8

Words and Music by Billie Eilish O'Connell
and Finneas O'Connell

Moderate Shuffle

Wait a min - ute. Let me fin - ish. I know you

don't care, but can you lis - ten?

I came com - mit - ted. Guess I o - ver - did it, poured my

heart out on a chain a - round my neck, and now it's miss - ing. Hmm.

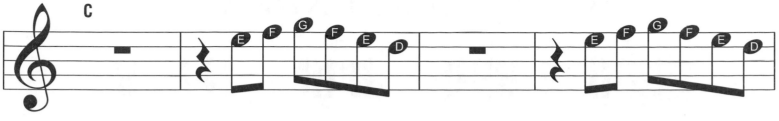

Da ba da da da du.          Da ba da da da du

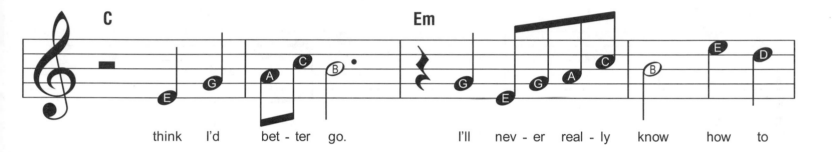

hmm.            Oh, _____ ooh ooh ooh.          So,    I

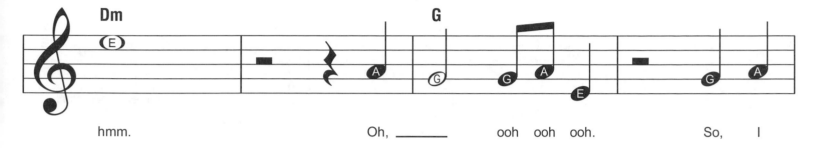

think   I'd   bet - ter   go.          I'll   nev - er   real - ly   know   how   to

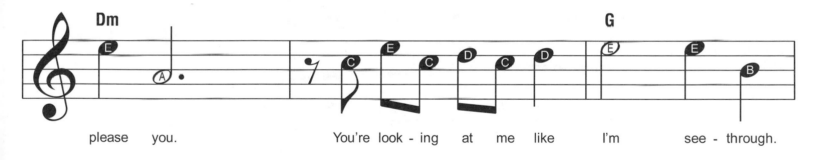

please   you.          You're   look - ing   at   me   like   I'm   see - through.

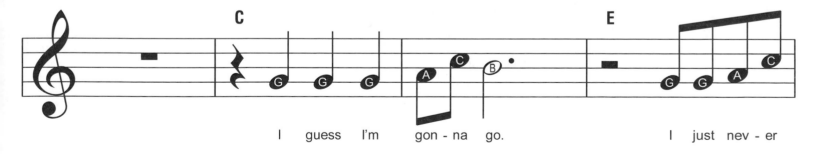

I   guess   I'm   gon - na   go.          I   just   nev - er

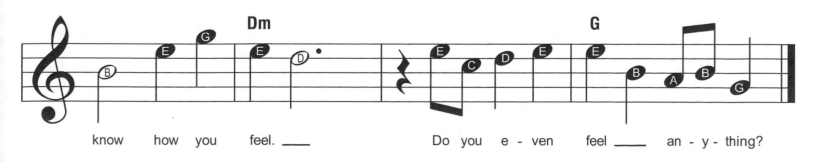

know   how   you   feel. ____          Do   you   e - ven   feel ____ an - y - thing?

# everything i wanted

Words and Music by Billie Eilish O'Connell
and Finneas O'Connell

19

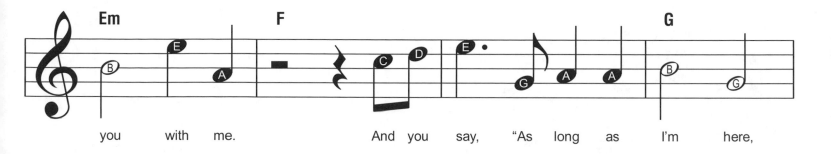

want - ed. But when I wake up, I see

you with me. And you say, "As long as I'm here,

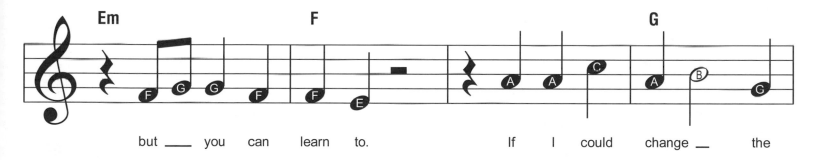

no ___ one can hurt you. Don't ___ wan - na lie here,

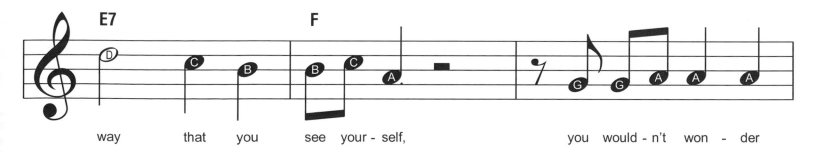

but ___ you can learn to. If I could change ___ the

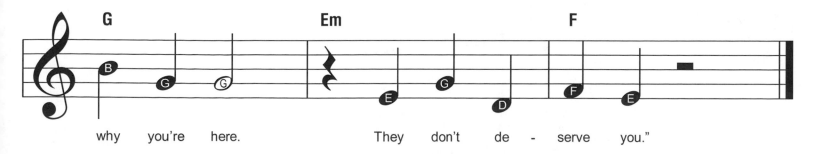

way that you see your - self, you would - n't won - der

why you're here. They don't de - serve you."

# hostage

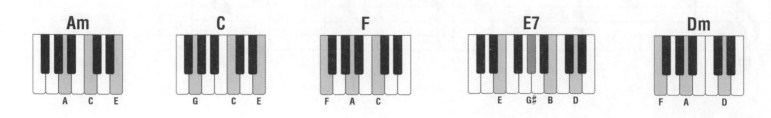

Words and Music by Billie Eilish O'Connell
and Finneas O'Connell

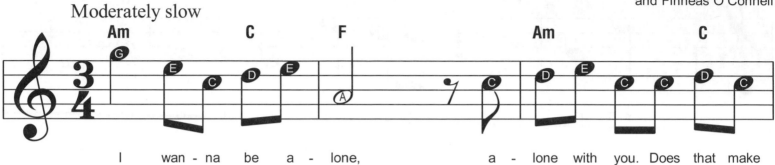

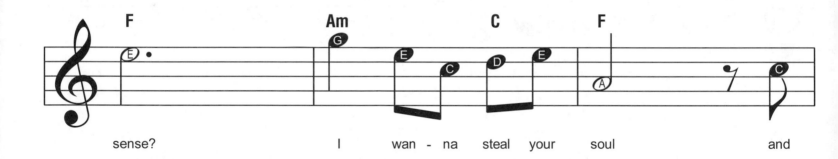

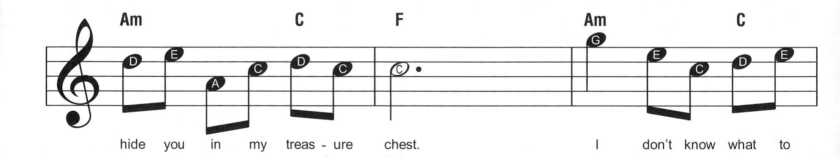

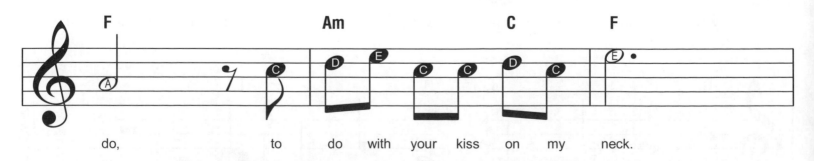

# i love you

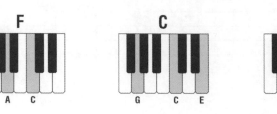
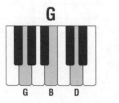

Words and Music by Billie Eilish O'Connell
and Finneas O'Connell

right          through.                    Ooh. _____

Mm. _____          May - be, won't you take it back? Say

you were tryin' to make me laugh, and          noth - ing has to change to - day. You

did - n't mean to say, "I love          you."                    I          love

you, _____          and          I          don't          want          to. _____

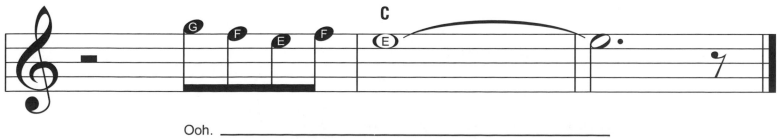

Ooh. _____

# idontwannabeyouanymore

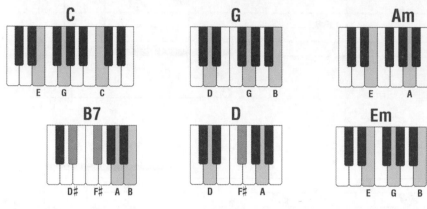

Words and Music by Billie Eilish O'Connell
and Finneas O'Connell

Lilting, in a slow 1

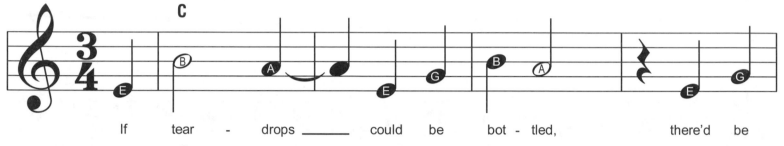

If tear - drops _____ could be bot - tled, there'd be

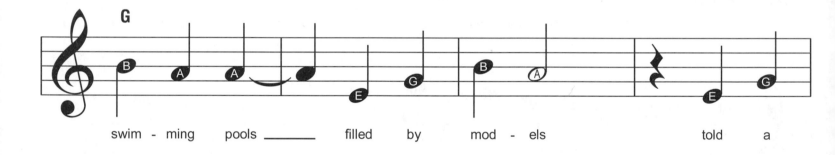

swim - ming pools _____ filled by mod - els told a

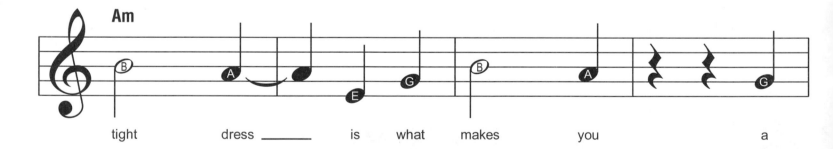

tight dress _____ is what makes you a

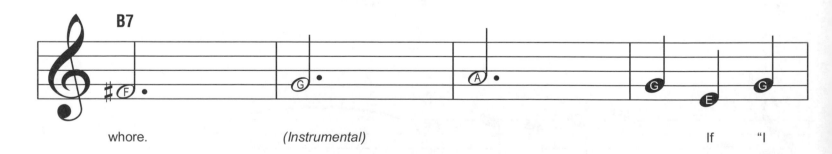

whore.    (Instrumental)    If "I

25

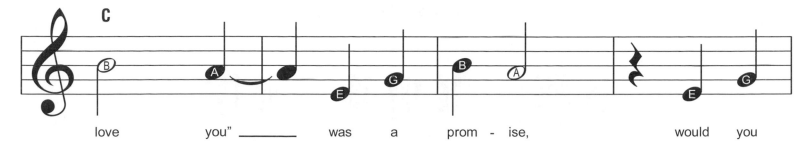

love you" _____ was a prom - ise, would you

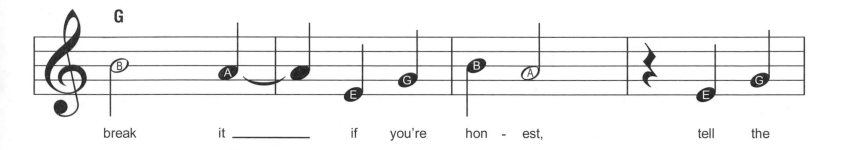

break it _____ if you're hon - est, tell the

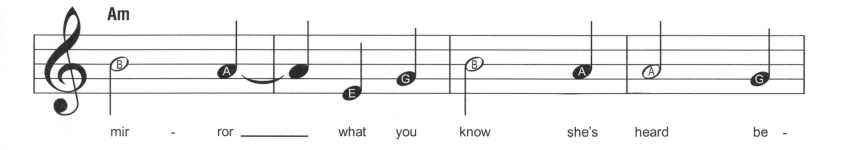

mir - ror _____ what you know she's heard be -

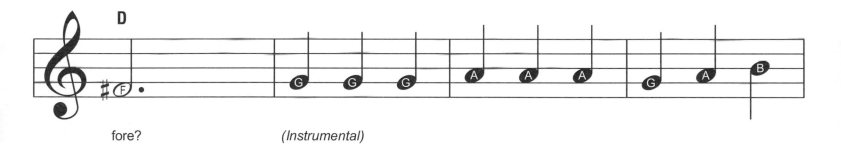

fore? *(Instrumental)*

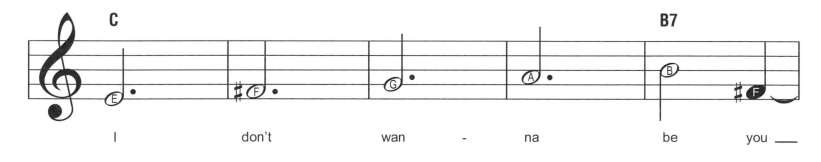

I don't wan - na be you ___

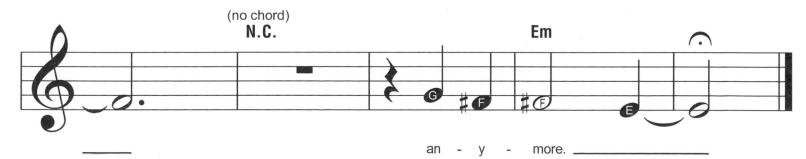

(no chord)

_____ an - y - more. _____

# ilomilo

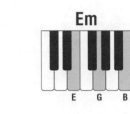

Words and Music by Billie Eilish O'Connell
and Finneas O'Connell

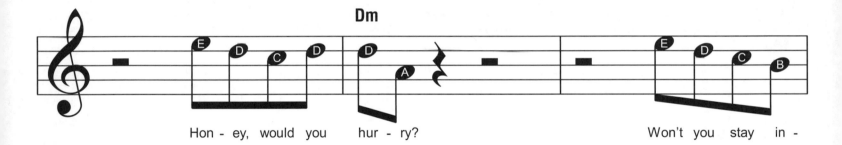

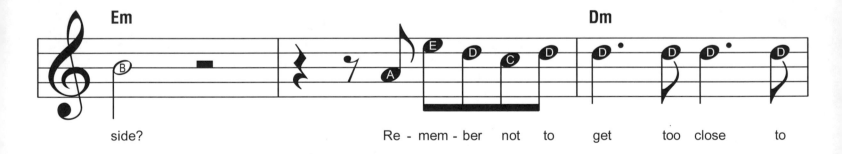

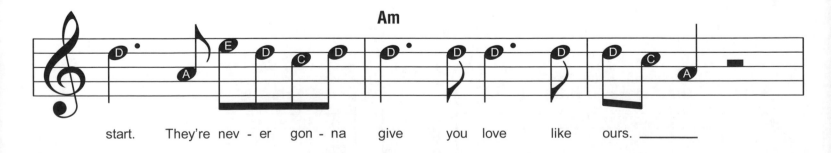

# listen before i go

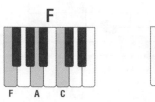
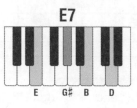
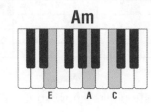
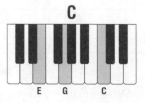

Words and Music by Billie Eilish O'Connell
and Finneas O'Connell

soon.        *(Instrumental)*        Sor - ry can't

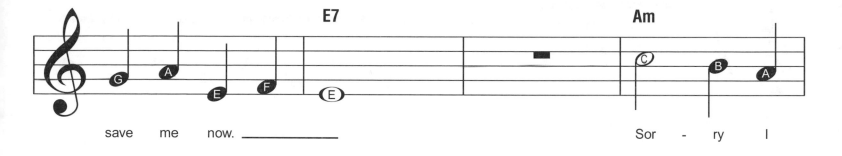

save me now. _____        Sor - ry I

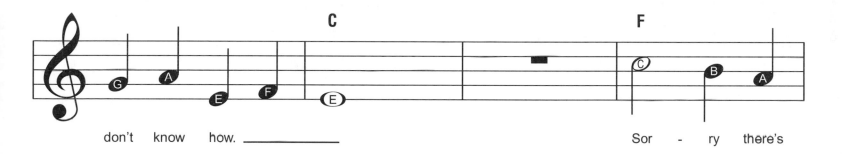

don't know how. _____        Sor - ry there's

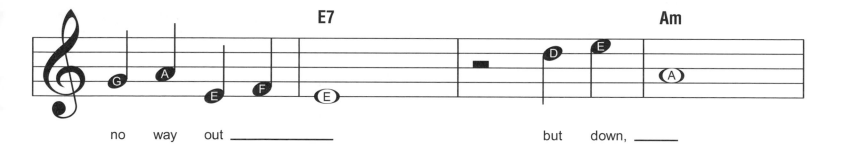

no way out _____        but down, _____

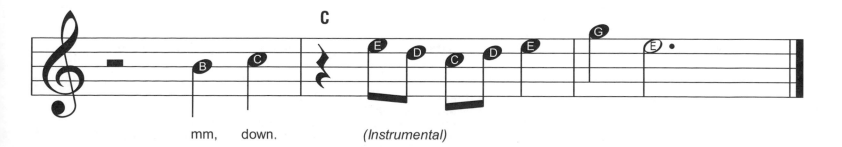

mm, down.        *(Instrumental)*

# lovely

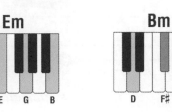

Words and Music by Billie Eilish O'Connell,
Finneas O'Connell and Khalid Robinson

# my strange addiction

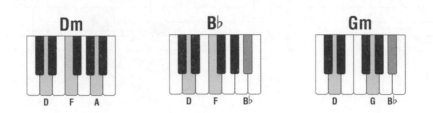

Words and Music by
Finneas O'Connell

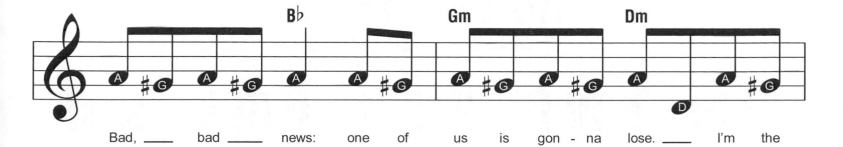

Bad, \_\_\_\_ bad \_\_\_\_ news: one of us is gon - na lose. \_\_\_\_ I'm the

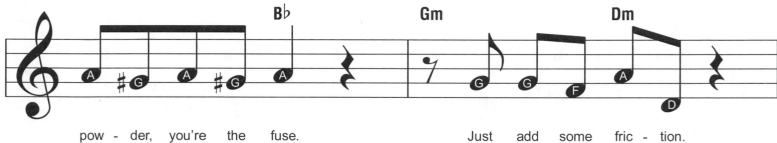

pow - der, you're the fuse. Just add some fric - tion.

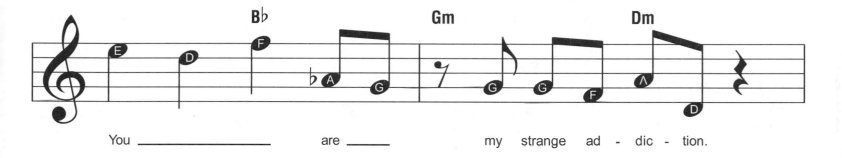

You _____ are \_\_\_\_\_ my strange ad - dic - tion.

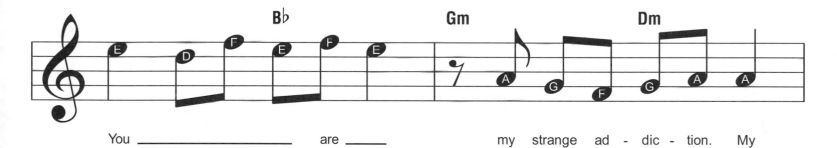

You _____ are \_\_\_\_\_ my strange ad - dic - tion. My

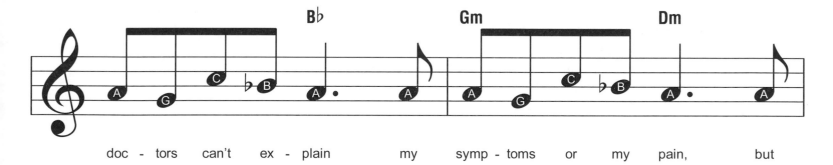

doc - tors can't ex - plain my symp - toms or my pain, but

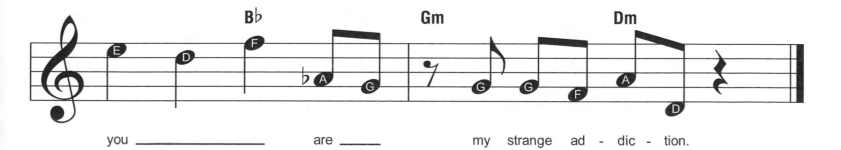

you _____ are \_\_\_\_\_ my strange ad - dic - tion.

# no time to die

## from NO TIME TO DIE

Words and Music by Billie Eilish O'Connell
and Finneas O'Connell

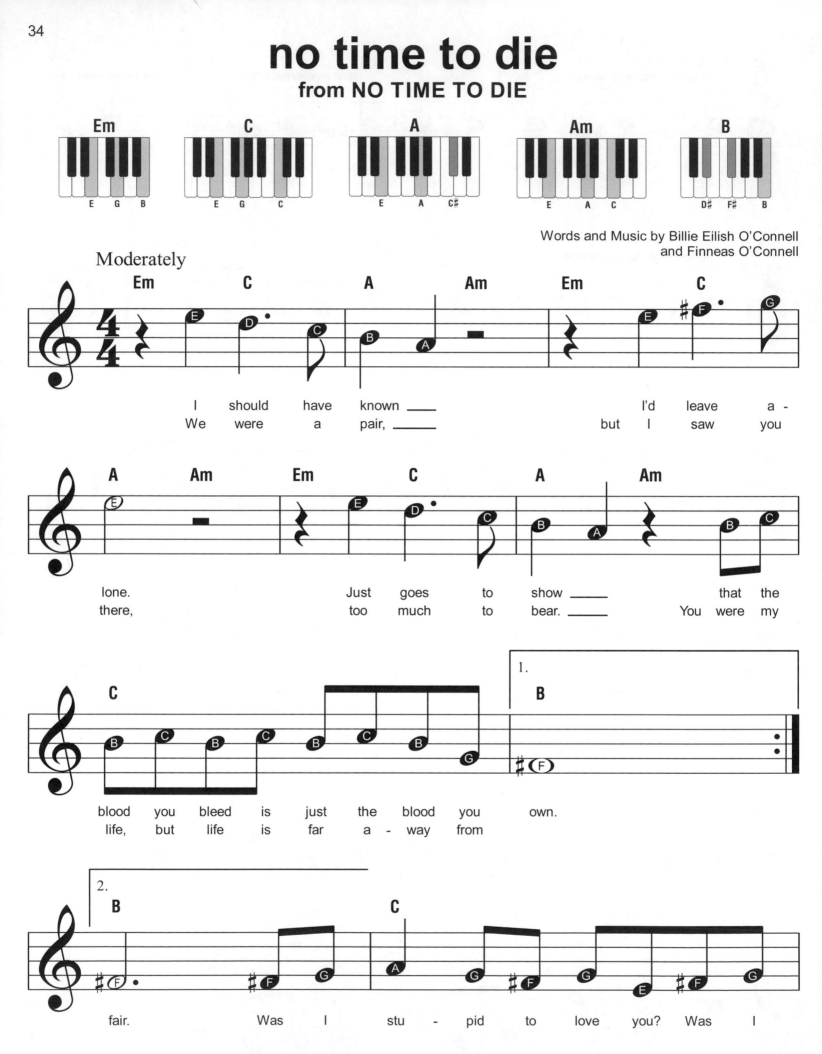

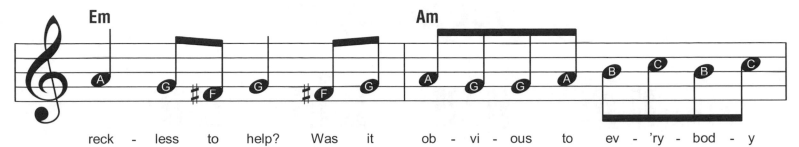

reck - less to help? Was it ob - vi - ous to ev - 'ry - bod - y

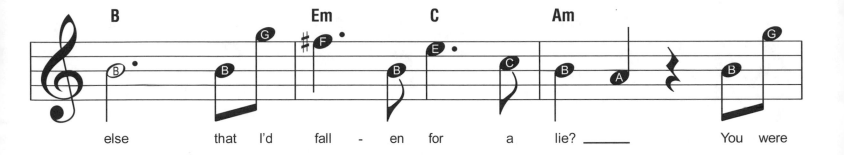

else that I'd fall - en for a lie? _____ You were

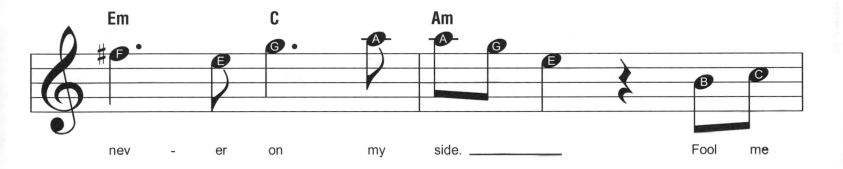

nev - er on my side. _____ Fool me

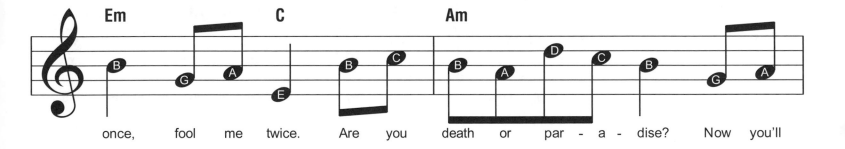

once, fool me twice. Are you death or par - a - dise? Now you'll

nev - er see me cry. There's just no time to die.

# ocean eyes

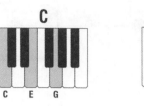
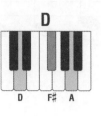
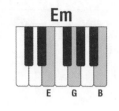
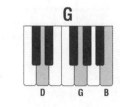

Words and Music by
Finneas O'Connell

Moderately

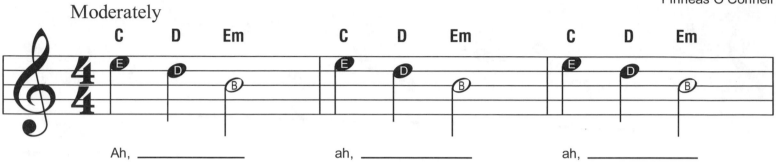

Ah, _____ ah, _____ ah, _____

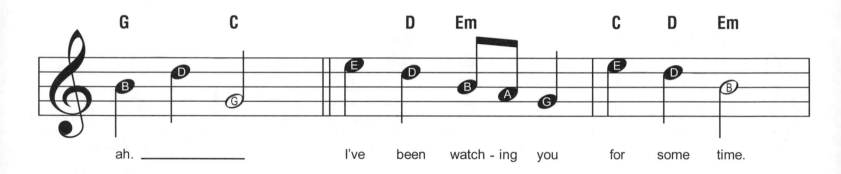

ah. _____ I've been watch - ing you for some time.

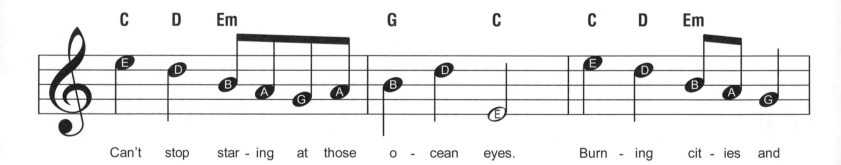

Can't stop star - ing at those o - cean eyes. Burn - ing cit - ies and

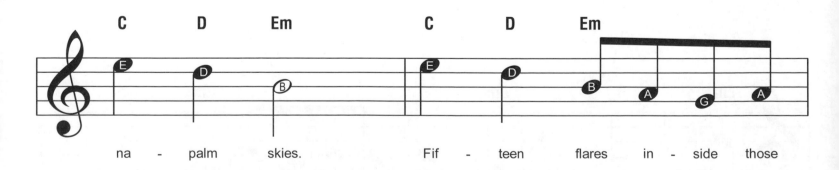

na - palm skies. Fif - teen flares in - side those

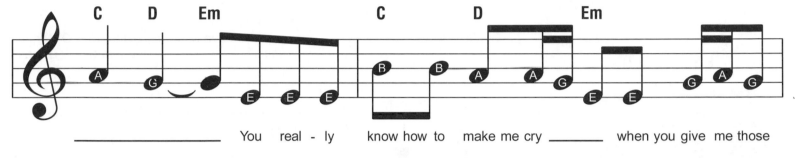

o - cean eyes, your o - cean eyes. No fair. _____

_____ You real - ly know how to make me cry _____ when you give me those

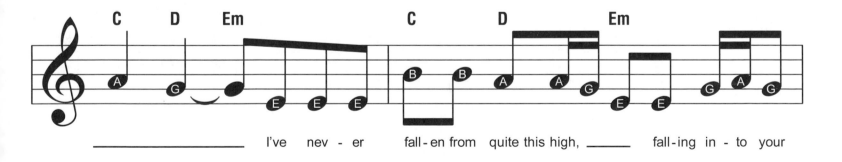

o - cean eyes. I'm scared. _____

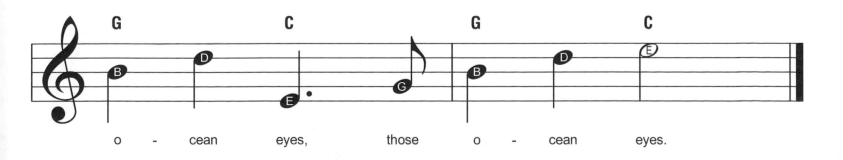

_____ I've nev - er fall - en from quite this high, _____ fall - ing in - to your

o - cean eyes, those o - cean eyes.

# party favor

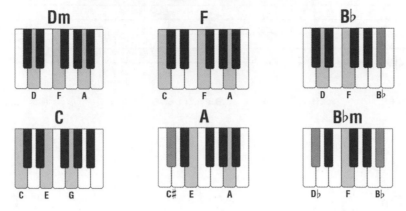

Words and Music by Billie Eilish O'Connell
and Finneas O'Connell

Folky Shuffle

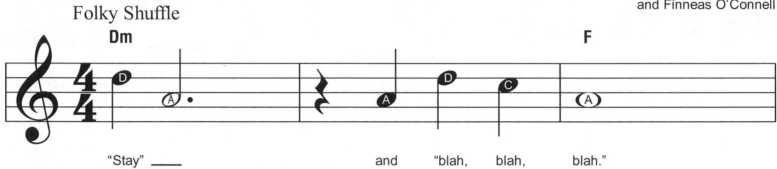

"Stay" ___ and "blah, blah, blah."

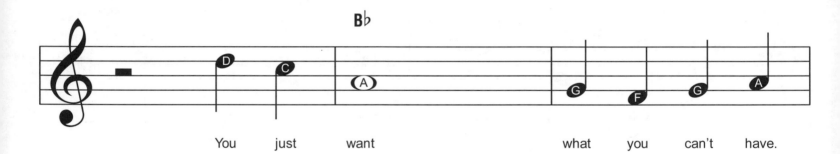

You just want what you can't have.

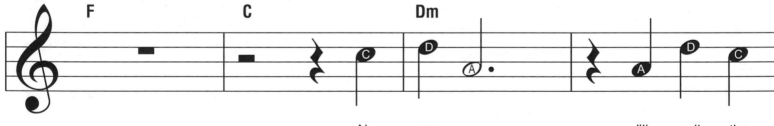

No way, ___ I'll call the

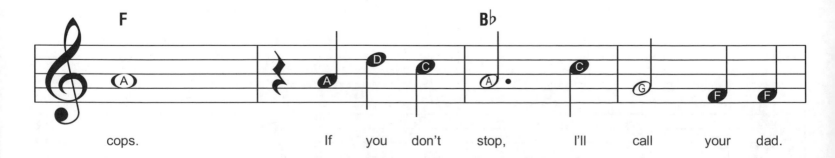

cops. If you don't stop, I'll call your dad.

# six feet under

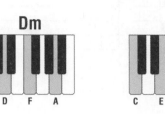
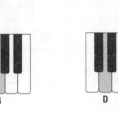
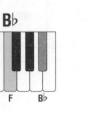

Words and Music by
Finneas O'Connell

Moderately slow half-time feel

Help. I lost my-self a-
Don't come back. It won't end

gain, but I re-mem-ber me
well, but I wish you'd tell me

you.
to.

Our love is

six feet un-der. I can't help but

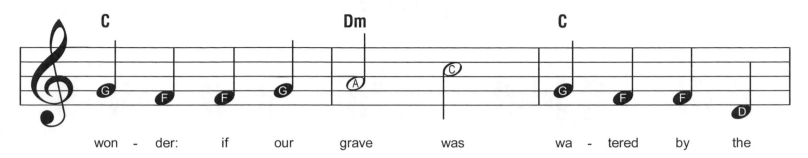

won - der: if our grave was wa - tered by the

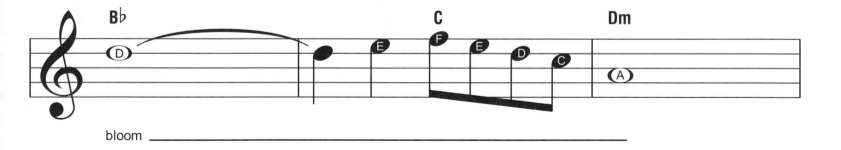

rain, would ros - es bloom? _____

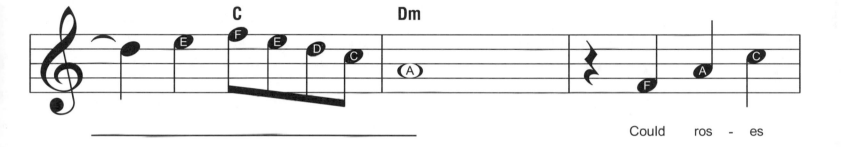

_____ Could ros - es

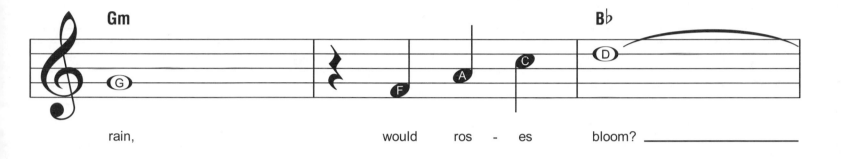

bloom _____

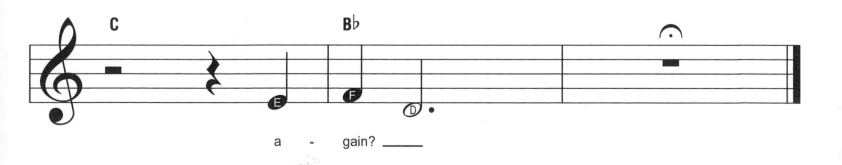

a - gain? _____

# watch

Words and Music by
Finneas O'Connell

# when the party's over

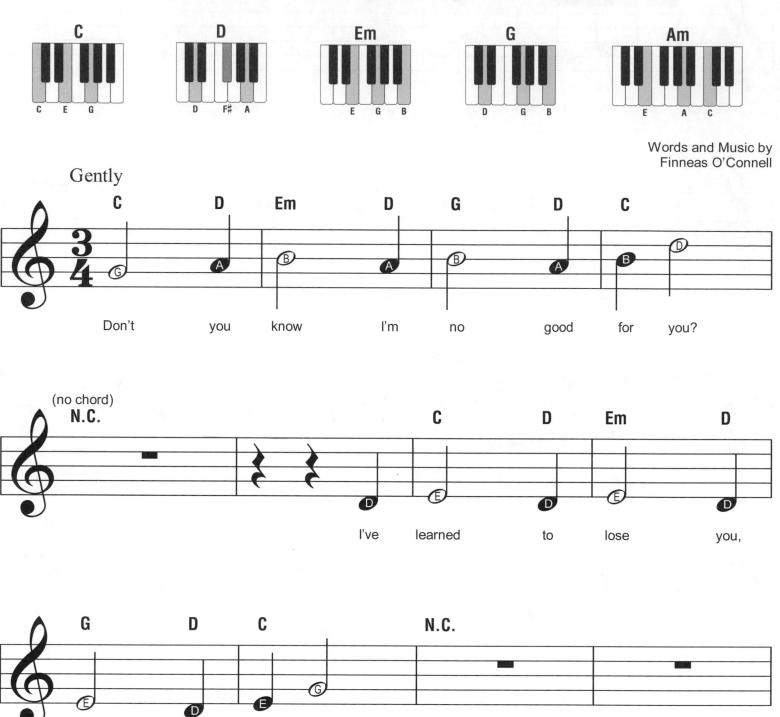

Words and Music by
Finneas O'Connell

Don't you know I'm no good for you?

I've learned to lose you,

can't af - ford to.

Tore my shirt to stop you bleed - ing.

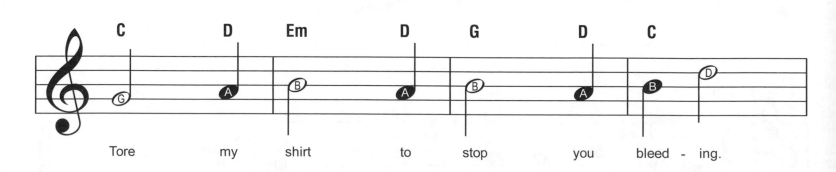

# wish you were gay

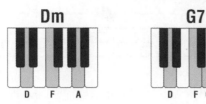
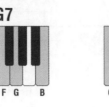
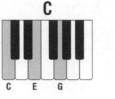
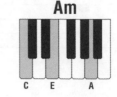

Words and Music by Billie Eilish O'Connell
and Finneas O'Connell

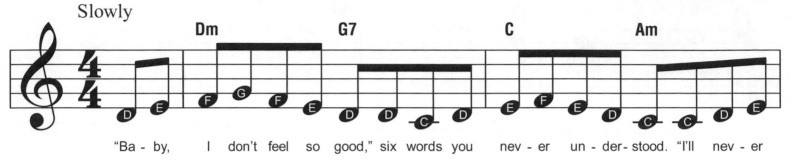

"Ba - by, I don't feel so good," six words you nev - er un - der - stood. "I'll nev - er

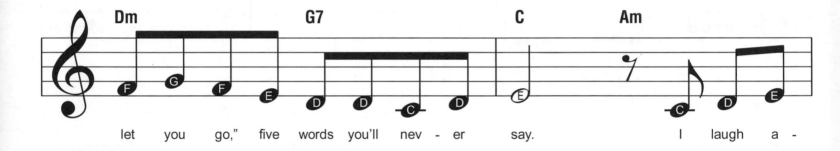

let you go," five words you'll nev - er say. I laugh a -

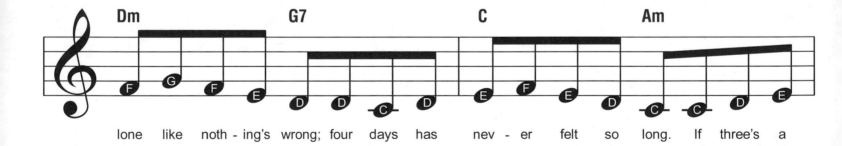

lone like noth - ing's wrong; four days has nev - er felt so long. If three's a

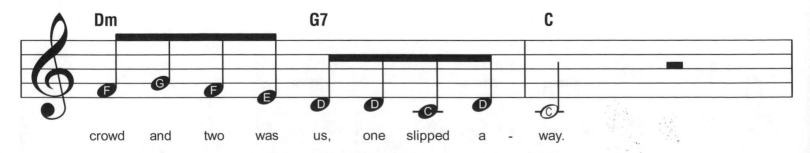

crowd and two was us, one slipped a - way.

**SUPER EASY SONGBOOK**

*It's super easy! This series features accessible arrangements for piano, with simple right-hand melody, letter names inside each note, and basic left-hand chord diagrams. Perfect for players of all ages!*

**ADELE**
00394705 22 songs.................$14.99

**THE BEATLES**
00198161 60 songs.................$15.99

**BEAUTIFUL BALLADS**
00385162 50 songs.................$14.99

**BEETHOVEN**
00345533 21 selections.............$9.99

**BEST SONGS EVER**
00329877 60 songs.................$16.99

**BROADWAY**
00193871 60 songs.................$15.99

**JOHNNY CASH**
00287524 20 songs.................$9.99

**CHART HITS**
00380277 24 songs.................$12.99

**CHRISTMAS CAROLS**
00277955 60 songs.................$15.99

**CHRISTMAS SONGS**
00236850 60 songs.................$15.99

**CHRISTMAS SONGS WITH 3 CHORDS**
00367423 30 songs.................$10.99

**CLASSIC ROCK**
00287526 60 songs.................$15.99

**CLASSICAL**
00194693 60 selections............$15.99

**COUNTRY**
00285257 60 songs.................$15.99

**DISNEY**
00199558 60 songs.................$15.99

**BOB DYLAN**
00364487 22 songs.................$12.99

**BILLIE EILISH**
00346515 22 songs.................$10.99

**FOLKSONGS**
00381031 60 songs.................$15.99

**FOUR CHORD SONGS**
00249533 60 songs.................$15.99

**FROZEN COLLECTION**
00334069 14 songs.................$12.99

**GEORGE GERSHWIN**
00345536 22 songs.................$9.99

**GOSPEL**
00285256 60 songs.................$15.99

**HIT SONGS**
00194367 60 songs.................$16.99

**HYMNS**
00194659 60 songs.................$15.99

**JAZZ STANDARDS**
00233687 60 songs.................$15.99

**BILLY JOEL**
00329996 22 songs.................$11.99

**ELTON JOHN**
00298762 22 songs.................$10.99

**KIDS' SONGS**
00198009 60 songs.................$16.99

**LEAN ON ME**
00350593 22 songs.................$10.99

**THE LION KING**
00303511 9 songs..................$9.99

**ANDREW LLOYD WEBBER**
00249580 48 songs.................$19.99

**MOVIE SONGS**
00233670 60 songs.................$15.99

**PEACEFUL MELODIES**
00367880 60 songs.................$16.99

**POP SONGS FOR KIDS**
00346809 60 songs.................$16.99

**POP STANDARDS**
00233770 60 songs.................$16.99

**QUEEN**
00294889 20 songs.................$10.99

**ED SHEERAN**
00287525 20 songs.................$9.99

**SIMPLE SONGS**
00329906 60 songs.................$15.99

**STAR WARS (EPISODES I-IX)**
00345560 17 songs.................$12.99

**HARRY STYLES**
01069721 15 songs.................$12.99

**TAYLOR SWIFT**
1192568 30 songs..................$14.99

**THREE CHORD SONGS**
00249664 60 songs.................$16.99

**TOP HITS**
00300405 22 songs.................$10.99

**WORSHIP**
00294871 60 songs.................$16.99

Disney characters and artwork TM & © 2021 Disney

Prices, contents and availability subject to change without notice.

**HAL•LEONARD®**
www.halleonard.com

0723
327